ADVANCE PRAISE

T0145592

"*Bolivia beyond the Impasse* is a b[...] Bolivia in the current conjuncture of global politics. Hardt and Mezzadra investigate Bolivia's society as a laboratory for the present and future of politics that involves innovation from above and below in their antagonistic cooperation. Their work brings about new political maps in which the tension between social conflict and the reconfiguration of institutions gives rise to critical possibilities for new politics of autonomy."

—**Massimiliano Tomba**, author of *Insurgent Universality: An Alternative Legacy of Modernity*

"In *Bolivia beyond the Impasse*, Michael Hardt and Sandro Mezzadra draw on years of solidaristic activism with the contentious 'process of change' in Bolivia, inaugurated electorally by the Evo Morales government following a wave of social movement insurgency at the outset of this century. Pointing to the impasse that the process faces today, their essay offers a sweeping contribution to the debate on the prospects for its renewal and radicalization. Written from a perspective of open and honest sympathy with the governments of Morales and his successor, Luis Arce, Hardt and Mezzadra are nonetheless attentive to a number of the limits and contradictions faced by these administrations, not least because the authors have spent time with clear-eyed Bolivian social movement activists and intellectuals on the ground. Perhaps the most important contribution of their intervention is that it reveals, once again, how the last two decades of concrete and particular social struggles in a landlocked Andean-Amazonian country are of pivotal and universal significance to the anticapitalist international left."

—**Jeffery R. Webber**, coauthor of *The Impasse of the Latin American Left*

"Bolivia's Movement for Socialism Party (MAS) has been a leading force in the struggle to build socialism, break the chains of imperialism, and dismantle racism. This timely book analyzes many of MAS's most important achievements, while also addressing impediments it has faced, including the 2019 coup d'état. In their analysis of the opportunities and challenges facing MAS and Bolivia's progressive social movements in the current conjuncture, Hardt and Mezzadra bring much-needed nuance to key debates around development, extractivism, and the relationship between movements and parties. They point to promising paths for development that could further challenge the international division of labor and advance the project of a just transition to sustainable energy."

—**Jennifer S. Ponce de León**, author of
Another Aesthetics is Possible: Arts of Rebellion
in the Fourth World War

"The Bolivian crucible, heated by revolution and counter-revolution alike, has much to teach us about the accomplishments and limitations of the first Pink Tide, and more importantly, about the prospects of a second. *Bolivia beyond the Impasse* gives us exactly what we need: a concise and even-handed analysis of what has happened, what is happening, and what radical possibilities can be glimpsed on the horizon."

—**Geo Maher**, author of *We Created Chávez*
and *Building the Commune*

BOLIVIA BEYOND THE IMPASSE

MICHAEL HARDT AND
SANDRO MEZZADRA

ISBN: 9781942173977 | eBook ISBN: 9781945335068
Library of Congress Number: 2023941753

10 9 8 7 6 5 4 3 2 1

Common Notions   Common Notions
c/o Interference Archive   c/o Making Worlds Bookstore
314 7th St.   210 S. 45th St.
Brooklyn, NY 11215   Philadelphia, PA 19104

www.commonnotions.org
info@commonnotions.org

Discounted bulk quantities of our books are available for organizing, educational, or fundraising purposes. Please contact Common Notions at the address above for more information.

Cover design by Josh MacPhee / Antumbra Design
Page Design and Typesetting by Suba Murugan

CONTENTS

PREFACE

IN THE FIRST decade of the new millennium, Latin American politics inspired and galvanized leftist activists and intellectuals around the globe. Although political developments took very different paths in Ecuador and Uruguay, Brazil and Venezuela, Bolivia and Argentina, they all nonetheless shared some central characteristics that made the region a beacon for those outside.

The extraordinary attraction was due, in part, to the way that Latin American social movements and governments announced their opposition to and autonomy from the neoliberal global order, in defiance of both US imperialist command and the control imposed by supranational institutions, such as the World Bank and the International Monetary Fund. Economic and political development would be determined independent of external dictations, often with explicitly anticapitalist initiatives. At a time when it appeared to many that there was, indeed, no alternative to the global neoliberal order, these Latin American movements declared and demonstrated that another world was possible, one that could be achieved by experimenting with forms of cooperation among governments and movements across the continent to create real conditions for autonomy within the global system.

The allure of these Latin American developments was also due to the original dynamics created between social movements and progressive governments. The majority of progressive governments elected in these years rode to power on the backs of the social movements, and many of the elected officials had themselves risen from leadership positions in the movements. The governments thus positioned themselves as expressions or representatives of the movements. The dynamics between social movements and the state were different in each country and in many cases the movements were coopted and depoliticized by the progressive governments, but, despite such difficulties, it was clear that a new terrain of struggle had been opened with extraordinary potential.

Bolivia played a special role in this Latin American wave of struggles. The attacks of the Bolivian movements against the neoliberal dictates of privatization were particularly fierce, especially in the 2000 war on water and the 2003 war on gas, which we will explain below. And at the time of the 2005 election as president of Evo Morales, a former leader of the mighty Cocaleros movement, the balance of power with the state seemed clearly to favor the social movements. In addition to this, however, the Bolivian situation was most importantly distinguished by the indigenous and anticolonial characteristics of the social movements and the newly elected government. Bolivia is a majority indigenous nation that had never, before Evo Morales, been led by a self-identified indigenous president. More importantly, throughout the social movements anticapitalism mixed inextricably with anticolonial ideals and indigenous organizational forms. An explicit mandate of the Morales government, driven in part by the movements, was to decolonize the Bolivian state and society. Many of the prime actors in the 2009 Constituent

Assembly attempted to put these decolonial ideals into practice, with results that were in some respects limited but nonetheless significant.

Much has changed in Latin America, of course, in the past two decades. During these years some progressive governments have been voted out of power for right-wing regimes; some social movements have been enveloped within the state, while others have simply lost their previous dynamism. Despite such setbacks, however, we still find it imperative to study and learn from today's Latin American social movements and political experiments. In some respects, the promise of the present is due to continuities with the previous phase through organizational achievements, widespread political demands, and progressive social habits that survive unchanged. But there have also been great new developments both in the emergence of powerful social movements, such as the feminist *Ni una menos*, and the election of progressive governments of various stripes in countries such as Colombia, Peru, Mexico, and Brazil. In all of this, Bolivia continues, in our view, to occupy a privileged position.

Given our conviction of the importance of Latin American and Bolivian political developments, we were thrilled to have the opportunity in August 2022 to meet in La Paz with a range of people directly engaged with the political and economic dynamics of the country. Many of our interlocutors were current or former government officials, both elected and administrative; others were activists in social movements; and some were scholars of the country and region. Those with whom we spoke ranged from strong critics of the government of Morales and García Linera to staunch defenders, but all were in the orbit of the Movement Toward Socialism (MAS) party and its progressive political projects.

In the following text, we attempt to sketch the primary characteristics of the current political, social, and economic situation of Bolivia. We seek to explain not only how this situation came about but also the obstacles that confront today's progressive forces and have led to an impasse, which has, since we originally wrote this text, been even further consolidated. Right-wing political and social forces, centered on the eastern city of Santa Cruz, continue to gain strength and constantly hinder or thwart progressive initiatives. Obstacles also arise from within, including the vexed question of leadership, which has increasingly surfaced in recent months between Morales as leader of the MAS party and Luis Arce as president of the government. We do not dwell on these obstacles, however, because we also recognize the extraordinary power and innovation that a new phase of political struggle in Bolivia could unleash, beyond the impasse. The current situation remains open to new political inventions rooted in the wide range of progressive and revolutionary forces both inside and outside the government and the MAS party.

Finally, while discussing the Bolivian situation we constantly keep one eye on the Latin American context because we firmly believe that, just as it was twenty years ago, many of today's most stubborn political and economic obstacles can only be overcome through mechanisms beyond national boundaries, by inventing effective mechanisms of regional cooperation. We are well aware that the path forward is not clear and that new and old right-wing forces constitute continuing and increasing threats throughout the region, from Brazil to Argentina, and from Colombia to Chile. Discovering how to defend against violent reactionary forces while furthering democratic initiatives and projects for liberation will be a key task for social movements and progressive governments. Despite all the threats and obstacles that feed the impasse, however, dynamics of insurgency and struggle continue to resonate and circulate throughout Latin America. This regional space of political action and innovation is where the potential for moving beyond the impasse is most promising.

INTRODUCTION

BOLIVIA'S POLITICAL, SOCIAL, and economic achievements since Evo Morales took office in 2006, and since the Movement Toward Socialism Party (MAS) has been the predominant force in national politics, are indicative of the accomplishments of the entire cycle of Latin American progressive governments (also known as the "pink tide") that began in the 2000s. (For further reading on the "pink tide" and other recommendations, see the bibliographical note at the end of the text.) Although small in geographical terms compared to many of its neighbors, Bolivia provided a privileged position for understanding the potential and results of progressive continental developments. Today, however, the political conjuncture in Latin America has changed. The socialist projects are constantly threatened by the aggressive and often violent oligarchic and right-wing forces, but they also face internal obstacles. There is widespread recognition, in particular, that, although they made great accomplishments, the dynamic of progressive policies that animated the left for over a decade has now been exhausted. Bolivia and the MAS are faced with an impasse, and therefore with the need to break with the policies of the long first phase and launch a new political, social, and economic project. In all these respects, Bolivia once again serves as a bellwether for gauging the obstacles and potential for further developments across the continent as a whole. The impasse in Bolivia, in fact, is symptomatic of not only the exhaustion of the first wave of progressive governments in Latin America which began in the early 2000s, but also of the challenges that must be overcome today, in order to realize a second wave across the continent.

At least since Cristina Fernández's 2015 election defeat in Argentina and Dilma Rousseff's 2016 impeachment in Brazil, many political observers have assumed that Latin America's cycle of progressive governments has come to an end; due to, in part, the limitations or failures of specific politicians and parties and, in part, the resurgent power of right-wing political forces. Also key was the fact that, in the wake of the financial crisis of 2007–2008, the terms of the global conjuncture have been dramatically different from those of the early 2000s. In particular, the commodity boom, which had laid the ground for the social policies of progressive governments in the region, has declined. The adverse conditions facing the progressive political projects were exploited by such figures as Mauricio Macri in Argentina and Jair Bolsonaro in Brazil, who combined neoliberalism with various degrees of populism and authoritarianism. According to many commentators, then, by the middle of the last decade, the pendulum of Latin American politics had swung to the right, creating a new neoliberal and authoritarian cycle in the region.

Such dire forecasts, however, proved to be mistaken. This is true, first of all, simply with respect to the continual emergence of struggles that have long made Latin America a continent of insurgency. The spread of feminist struggles across the region, spurred by the extraordinary, successful campaign for abortion rights in Argentina, involved Indigenous, Afrodescendent, and popular movements, creating new forms of intersectional struggles. In October 2019, the Chilean uprising created the conditions for putting an end to the legacy of Pinochet and to start a process of deep transformation of the country through the election of a constituent assembly (even though the referendum on the constitution failed to pass in September 2022). Also in 2019, popular revolts in Ecuador, with huge Indigenous participation, compelled President Lenín Moreno to withdraw the *paquetazo*, a set of neoliberal measures. In May 2021, finally, a mass social movement against a fiscal reform in Colombia gave way to a general mobilization against the prevailing social and political system that created the conditions for wider change.

The 2021 election of Gabriel Boric in Chile, and the 2022 victory of Gustavo Petro and Francia Márquez in Colombia, are obviously connected to this history of struggles and uprisings, and they suggest the possibility of a second wave of progressive movements in Latin America, to which Lula's narrow victory in Brazil gives some added force. We are well aware of the stiff challenges facing each of these progressive governments and also the political compromises they may be forced to accept, but that should not lead us to discount the potential opened up by their victories. All of the progressive governments have to confront the same challenge facing Bolivia that we mentioned above; namely, to invent new social and economic programs, which both mark a rupture from the progressive projects of the first wave and, at the same time, extend further their antineoliberal, decolonial, anti-imperialist, socialist initiatives, while opening new spaces for feminist, Indigenous, and environmental projects. In short, they have to take stock of the impasse and the exhaustion of political productivity that led to the end of several progressive governments and that continue to haunt present actors.

Another aspect of the first wave of progressive governments that should be relaunched and redefined is the continental vision of cooperation in *nuestra América* that was initiated, in particular, by Chávez and Lula and that translated onto plans of monetary, logistical, and infrastructural integration. In the current multipolar and conflictual world, a new politics of regional integration in Latin America would be vitally important; it would help to manage relations within the world market and multiply the efforts to establish new developmental paths in the countries involved. While national factors are surely important, an emphasis on the regional dimension may be key today to produce a breakthrough, and to open a new political cycle for the left. Currently, however, there are no strong proposals of continental cooperation on the table, and the national viewpoint presently prevails in the region.

This brings us back to the importance of Bolivia within this wider picture of Latin American politics. The government of Evo Morales and Álvaro García Linera, elected in 2005 in the wake of the water and gas "wars" of the early 2000s, made crucial contributions, as we said, to the first wave of progressive governments. Notwithstanding the damage caused by the coup of November 2019, and the "de facto" right-wing government that ruled for the following year, the MAS was able to win a landslide victory in 2020, and continues to hold the government under President Luis Arce and Vice President David Choquehuanca. This amazing continuity over almost two decades provides a privileged standpoint for understanding the history of progressive governments and the articulation between the first and the incipient second wave. This is true both for the successes accomplished since 2006, as well as for the limits of those processes and the need for new directions and a new project. We have thus been particularly attuned throughout our research and our conversations with those in government and social movements, to indications of Bolivia moving beyond the impasse. At stake here, is the possibility of a renewed phase of radical and reformist politics that is able to open spaces for revolutionary action at the national and continental levels.

A BALANCE SHEET OF ADVANCES AND OBSTACLES UP TO THE COUP

BEFORE ANALYZING ITS limitations and difficulties, one should take a step back and recognize the extent to which, since taking office in 2006, the government of Morales and García Linera successfully transformed Bolivia's political structures and social relations. It did so despite recurrent efforts to block this process by powerful and often violent oligarchic and right-wing forces, which are generally located geographically in the "half-moon" of provinces in the eastern part of the country, particularly in Santa Cruz, the center of the country's agro-industry sectors. The power of reactionary forces, already apparent in the 2008 "secessionist" crisis, came fully into view in the process of the 2019 coup, but their power has been a constant pressure throughout the decades of progressive government.

One of the greatest successes of the government has been the dramatic empowerment of Indigenous populations. Bolivia is a majority Indigenous country, with thirty-six recognized ethnic groups, of which Aymara and Quechua are the largest. Although there are no precise figures regarding race and ethnicity, in part due to a long history of racial mixture and variations of self-identification, roughly 60 percent to 80 percent can be considered Indigenous. Indigenous empowerment can be recognized, first of all, within the arena and structures of government. The symbolic importance of Evo Morales being the first Indigenous president should not be underestimated. Along with the president, there has been a massive influx of Indigenous populations in the parliament and other representative institutions as well as throughout the institutions of government administration at national, municipal, and local levels. There has been a dramatic transformation, in short, of who runs the governmental apparatuses. Indigenous empowerment in government has also been facilitated by redesigning the structures of the state, most notably by the Constitution passed in 2009, that now designates the country as a "plurinational state," no longer using the term "republic," which is associated with the lasting colonial elements of the previous, white-ruled governments. The Wiphala flag, consisting of many cascading blocks of color, that is often coupled with the traditional tricolor national banner, has come to symbolize the Indigenous and plurinational nature of the country. The elaborate system of autonomies laid out in the Constitution to establish the self-determination of Indigenous communities is an ambitious plan to reorganize the state, although to date only a small portion of the plan has been implemented. One element at stake here is to create a constitutional system outside of the traditional frame of sovereignty.

Economic and cultural advances have also been important parts of Indigenous empowerment. Aymara groups, in particular, have emerged as major forces in commercial relations. Peasant unions and coca growers are given more prominent voice and their economic interests have direct influence on government. More generally, the government has aided in a revalorization of Indigenous identities, seeking to undo the centuries-long cultural structures of subordination and subservience. Unsurprisingly, with Indigenous empowerment and affirmation has come, too, resentment by white populations at their loss of privilege, to which we will return shortly.

Many other major successes of the government intersect or overlap with the empowerment of Indigenous populations and the indigenization of society and the state. The socialist government, for instance, has used proceeds from national industries to fund health and education initiatives as well as subsidies and other anti-poverty programs that have dramatically lifted the living conditions and economic prospects of the poorest populations, which are most often Indigenous. State funds have also been dedicated to large and small infrastructure projects. One program that holds particular promise, in our view, is opening access to education and, in particular, making public education including university free of charge for all Bolivians.

Along with these considerable successes accomplished during the fifteen years of the MAS government, several difficult political problems have emerged at the level of party and state. The accumulation of these obstacles has led to a kind of inertia of the social forces that stand behind the government and has created an impasse of the political project.

One set of problems revolves around the tendency toward a centralization of power in the party and in the executive institutions of the state. The election of Evo Morales in December 2005, as we said, was made possible by a wide array of powerful social movements, most of which were strongly characterized by Indigenous politics. The struggles of the Cocaleros, in which Morales himself was a central protagonist, the 2000 movement against the privatization of water centered in Cochabamba, and the 2003 movements against the privatization of natural gas centered in El Alto, were some of the most visible high points of the range of struggles that eventually supported Evo's election. Once elected, however, the government effectively reorganized these antagonistic social forces. In large part, the social movements that had struggled against the ruling powers were brought within the governmental structures. Many central activists found positions within governmental agencies, and key social movements became institutionalized within the state. To some degree, this process involved empowering those social movements by giving them access to governmental structures; and to an equal degree, the process coopted the movements within the state's own projects. However one evaluates this complex process, and we will return later to analyze further the relations between the state and social movements, there has undeniably been a tendency to centralize power within the state and, further, within the executive branch. There has developed, in fact, a strong overlap between the leadership of the party and that of the state.

The process of centralization has gone hand in hand with bureaucratization, both of state structures and the social movements that have been incorporated into them. Many activists who had engaged in antagonistic struggles prior to 2006 and many who continue to be active in social movements experience this as a process of depoliticization and demobilization. It is open to debate whether this depoliticization is an inevitable consequence of progressive forces gaining state power. At the least, one can say that, as the social movements have increasingly taken on administrative functions, they have reduced their antagonistic capacities—not only their power to challenge government policies but also their ability to defend the government against the threats of right-wing politics and violence, which we will see, shortly, with regard to the 2019 coup.

Another unresolved problem faced by the government regards how to respond to the demands of the oligarchy and the various right-wing political forces. This is a complex question that cannot be easily summarized, but the Morales government in many cases attempted to de-escalate conflicts with right-wing powers and avoid direct and violent confrontations. In many respects, the government pursued a strategy of accommodation, granting some demands of right-wing political leaders and forces, and preserving their economic interests in the framework of what Gracia Linera calls "Andean-Amazonian capitalism," in the hope of defusing or avoiding conflicts. During the 2019 coup, however, it became abundantly clear that such a strategy of accommodation could not successfully calm right-wing forces.

Some of these obstacles are illustrated by the 2011 conflict over construction of a highway through the TIPNIS Indigenous territory and national park in Bolivia's eastern lowlands. In some respects, the project presented a traditional political conflict: a modernization infrastructure project designed to integrate the country—the highway would connect the Amazonian region in Beni province to the central city of Cochabamba and the Andean region—was at odds with the interests of Indigenous populations and environmental concerns. Morales' personal engagement and central authority was highlighted, especially when national police brutally repressed an Indigenous-led march protesting the highway in August 2011—a discordant image with the police repression of Indigenous protests that Morales himself led less than a decade earlier. The question of Indigenous interests in this case, however, is not as clear as it might at first seem. The TIPNIS clash, in fact, highlighted differences and conflicts *among* Indigenous groups in Bolivia. The majority of Bolivia's Indigenous population, as we said, resides in the Andean highlands and belongs to the Aymara and Quechua ethnic groups. The lowland ethnic groups are much smaller, including the Moxeño-Trinitario, Yuracaré, and Chimáne peoples that collectively hold title to the TIPNIS park as ancestral homeland. Significant Indigenous populations, then, in particular those that would benefit economically from the new highway, such as peasants and coca growers in Cochabamba, were largely in favor of the project. Without attempting to evaluate the many political complexities of the project and the conflict, the TIPNIS confrontation demonstrated, in addition to the difficulties posed by Evo's own authority, the challenge of political and economic conflicts among Indigenous groups that emerged? in the period of great Indigenous empowerment.

Some obstacles are also illustrated by the government's failed attempt in 2017 to reform the national penal code with respect to abortion. The government's strategy was not to legalize or even decriminalize abortion directly through judicial or legislative action, as in other Latin American countries, but instead to multiply from two to fourteen the legal motives permitted for terminating a pregnancy, which would effectively approximate legalization. Feminist movements have a different history and composition in Bolivia than in other Latin American countries. In Bolivia, many feminist activists lament that NGOs and middle-class populations are still seen as occupying the primary space of "feminism," a fact that has limited the power for reform. The primary reason the reform failed was that the government felt it did not have sufficient social support to challenge the conservative forces aligned against it, including the Catholic and Evangelical Churches as well as the powerful associations of medical doctors. The government withdrew the reform proposal in January 2018.

These problems and obstacles are some of the reasons for a sense of stagnation or impasse regarding the government's political project. Opinions differ about when the impasse began, but there seems to be near universal agreement that the first great period of political transformation initiated by the MAS and the Morales government has reached a point of exhaustion, and that a new endeavor will be necessary to relaunch the process.

COUP D'ÉTAT

IT IS WORTH recounting in some detail the October 2019 election and the subsequent coup that overthrew the government and nullified the election results, since these events are especially significant for future developments in the country. Morales and García Linera, the MAS candidates for president and vice president, arrived at the election significantly weakened for several reasons. We have already mentioned the sense of exhaustion of the political program, the increasing bureaucratization of the state, and the relative depoliticization of social movements that support the MAS. Also significant was the fallout from the 2016 referendum, which the government promoted, to modify the Constitution and abrogate term limits so as to allow Morales and García Linera to run for another term. The referendum was rejected by popular vote, which could have been taken as a challenge to the MAS to innovate not only its political personnel but also its understanding of leadership. Subsequently, however, the Supreme Court overruled the constitutional term limits, allowing Morales and García Linera to run for election again, despite the fact that the referendum had been rejected. The failed referendum and skirting its results weakened support for Morales and García Linera and increased their political vulnerability. Like the TIPNIS controversy, the referendum process not only eroded the government's base, but also emboldened right-wing parties and politicians to use the incident as evidence of their claims of election fraud, which they began long before the 2019 election took place.

Despite these weaknesses, however, Morales and García Linera won the October 2019 election convincingly. There were initial reports of voting "irregularities" by the right-wing parties and some international observers, but subsequent studies verified the results and confirmed there were no significant problems. Nonetheless, in several Bolivian cities, including Potosí and Cochabamba, electoral "fraud" was denounced even before polling stations closed. On the following day the growing lead of the MAS candidates in the official vote count was taken as proof of fraud although it was, in reality, due to the late influx of results from rural areas where the party is traditionally strong. At issue was not only the fact that Morales received the most votes, but also the margin of his lead. According to Bolivian voting regulations, when a candidate receives over 10 percent more votes than the second candidate in the first round—Morales took 47 percent and the right-wing Carlos Mesa took 36.5 percent—a run-off election is not necessary. Morales thus should have been declared the victor, avoiding run-off by a small margin.

The right-wing parties and social forces, however, continued to claim fraud and refused to accept the results, with significant backing from international institutions like the Organization of American States and the European Union. Claims of fraud and operations of social disruption, which had been planned well before the election, were orchestrated by right-wing politicians. Government election offices were set on fire by crowds chanting "fraud" and election workers were arrested and threatened. There were also right-wing protests and strikes, particularly in Santa Cruz and Cochabamba, that included violence against

MAS supporters and Indigenous people, including women in traditional dress, some of which was conducted by paramilitary gangs.

EVENTUALLY, AFTER WEEKS of considerable confusion and social conflict, significant portions of the police and armed forces expressed their support of the right-wing protests against the MAS. Many leftist forces were ready to come out in the streets, to fight and defend the government, despite the relative demo-bilization and depoliticization of the previous years, but Morales discouraged them from doing so. On November 10, Morales announced that he would agree to hold new elections to appease the right-wing opposition, but soon afterward on the same day, to the surprise and dismay of many supporters ready to defend the government, he resigned from office. Along with Morales, the vice president and the presidents of both the Senate and the Chamber of Deputies (all of them MAS Party members) also resigned, evacuating the constitutional line of succession. The group of MAS leaders who had resigned arrived in Mexico, after a harrowing journey, and later Argentina for an extended period of exile. Jeanine Añez, the second vice president of the Senate, a relatively minor figure in the right-wing political universe and former television presenter, declared herself next in line for the presidency (without any clear constitutional basis). With the support of the police and the military, Añez formed a "de facto" government.

It is not entirely clear why Morales decided to resign when he did. He may have calculated that, especially considering the defection of the armed forces, the balance of power was not favor-able, and furthermore that he and other MAS leaders were in physical danger. More importantly, it seems likely that Morales recognized that, if allowed to continue on its path, the course of events would lead toward civil war. Temporarily removing himself and his government from the scene may have been the only means to prevent that deadly and destructive outcome, although there continues to be a strong disagreement regarding Morales' decision among social movements and sectors of the MAS that criticize the lack of preparation and mobilization to respond to the attack of the right.

This sequence of events should be understood as a coup d'état, in our view, even though it does not match the conventional image of tanks and war planes descending on La Moneda Palace, and even though Morales and the MAS leadership resigned and fled the country. (Some Bolivians, including a small number of leftist critics of the government, refuse to use the term.) The fact that the elected government was deposed by the threat of force, orchestrated by right-wing political forces in collaboration with military leaders, sufficiently fits the definition of a coup.

In any case, the Añez government was a disaster in many respects. First of all, the "de facto" government was not able to unite the right-wing forces, and thus failed to develop any coherent political project. Furthermore, popular resistance to the "de facto" government by MAS supporters was strong and the government response was brutal. Añez issued a decree that in the repression of protestors, members of the police and the military would no longer face criminal liability, effectively giving them free rein. Her decree was quickly followed by mass arrests and government massacres—notably when soldiers and police killed protesters in Sacaba near Cochabamba and in Senkata in El Alto. One particularly significant symbolic event captured on video during the first days of the coup was the burning of the Wiphala flag by police and right-wing forces in front of the Government Palace in La Paz, making the racist face of the coup explicit. Indeed, the fear that white supremacy could be eroded or even overthrown was the most solid thread that held together, however tenuously, the various right-wing forces.

The invalidated November 2019 elections were initially scheduled to be conducted again in May 2020, but Añez, claiming that COVID restrictions would interfere, postponed them until September 2020. When the election finally took place, after mass mobilizations that became particularly radical in August, the MAS Party won a landslide victory. With The presidential and vice-presidential candidates, Luis Arce and David Choquehuanca, received over 55 percent of the vote, compared to less than 29 percent for the second-place finisher, Carlos Mesa. The MAS leaders in exile soon returned to Bolivia and Evo Morales reassumed Party leadership. In March 2021, Añez was arrested along with several of her former ministers and members of the military high command. She was charged with conspiracy, sedition, terrorism, and falsely assuming the presidency, and is currently serving a ten-year prison term. Luis Fernando Camacho, the governor of Santa Cruz and one of the most prominent right-wing politicians, was arrested in December 2022 and charged for his role in the coup.

The Arce/Choquehuanca government was successful in its efforts to stabilize the MAS Party and the Bolivian government, especially during the first two years of its mandate. It proceeded with pragmatic government policies, such as a vigorous and successful campaign to institute COVID protocols and increase vaccinations. Arce is widely regarded as an effective administrator who skillfully resolves conflicts within the party, among different sectors of the government, and in the country at large. It is equally widely recognized, however, that the Arce government is not prepared to launch a new political project. Hence the political impasse, which was already a primary feature before the coup, remains now with the MAS government back in power, exacerbated by increasing tensions between the presidency and party leadership.

In order to analyze more closely both the successes of the Bolivian government and the nature of its political impasse, with an eye toward the potential for future developments, we will investigate three primary areas, which overlap to a great degree. We begin by exploring the possibilities for alternative economic developments, with a focus on the long traditions of extractivist practices and the extent to which they have been modified. Secondly, we look more closely at the transformations of Indigenous politics, including the empowerment of and emerging conflicts among Indigenous populations, along with expressions of white resentment at the loss of privilege. The final arena is expressly political, that is, the relation between the state and social movements. Our vision in all these fields is oriented toward potential for extending and going beyond the political projects of the last fifteen years, in order to relaunch the progressive project on a new basis, beyond the impasse. And we are particularly attuned, whenever possible, to openings for regional and continental cooperation that could be key to initiating such a new phase.

PART I
ALTERNATIVE ECONOMIC DEVELOPMENT AND NEW TERRAINS OF STRUGGLE: EXTRACTIVISM AND LITHIUM

IN BOLIVIA, AS in several other Latin American countries, extraction has long been a central pillar of economic development, dominating colonial and postcolonial economies with extreme forms of violence and exploitation. The extractivist economy, however, despite this tragic past and notwithstanding widespread contemporary social, economic, and ecological critiques, remains central in Bolivia's present economy and will, inevitably, have a key role in any future project for alternative economic development. Analyzing the current Bolivian situation provides an excellent opportunity for analyzing the critical discourses regarding both extraction and development.

The case of lithium, which we will explore more fully later or shortly, provides particularly clear insight into this seeming contradiction. One could oppose lithium mining together with other forms of extraction, including oil, gas, coal, metals, and monocultural agriculture, insofar as they all carry far-reaching ecological and social damages. And yet, lithium and particularly lithium batteries are essential to most conceptions of a society with less reliance on or even free from carbon-based energy. In this respect, lithium may thus constitute an exception in the realm of extractivist practices: a form of extraction that could provide a basis for alternative economic and social development. In a way, one can say that extraction in its traditional forms built the economic basis for the first phase of the MAS government and extractivism is therefore involved in the processes that led to its impasse. Perhaps new forms of extraction, however, with lithium at the center, could generate a breakthrough in the field of development, connected to wider social and political transformations. In fact, we are fully aware of the fact that alternative development cannot be reduced to technological innovations like the lithium batteries.

Before further exploring the case of lithium and the question of economic development, however, we should emphasize how much, in Bolivia, specters of the extractivist past weigh heavily on the present. In the mid-sixteenth century, the "Cerro Rico de Potosí" provided silver that consolidated the Spanish Empire as a global power, while condemning thousands of Indigenous people to toil under the system of forced labor known as the *mita*. Mining and the export of raw materials for the world market, along with the exploitation of Indigenous communities in the agrarian forced labor regime of the *haciendas*, remained key to the economy of postcolonial Bolivia after the establishment of the republic in 1825, despite a decades, long depression of the silver, mining industry in the mid-nineteenth century. In the 1860s and 1870s, when the lack of silver mining was compensated by a boom of other metals, such as tin, foreign capital poured into the Bolivian mining sector, initially from Chile and Britain, and continued in the wake of Chile's 1883 victory over Bolivia in the "War of the Pacific." Technology and machinery employed for the modernization of the production process in mines were imported, while new infrastructures (including railways) were built to facilitate export. In the first half of the twentieth century the country was dominated by a small number of Bolivian "robber baron" mine owners. Finally, the armed uprising of miners led to Bolivia's 1952 National Revolution, which put an end to the "oligarchic system" and the corresponding forms of domination in the mines, but extractive activities continued nonetheless to be a defining feature of Bolivian economy. In the following decades, characterized by a succession of civil and military (as well as "military-peasant") governments, the state came to play prominent roles in the extractive sector. In the long "neoliberal" decade (1985–2000) those roles were radically downsized, private interests were restored, and the power of the miners (the main actors behind the powerful union, the *Central Obrera Boliviana*), was radically diminished. Extraction (of minerals, hydrocarbons, and now increasingly soy in Santa Cruz) continued to shape the economic landscape of the country, with foreign-owned corporations often constituting the lion's share.

Despite this tragedy-filled and in many respects disastrous history of extractivist economic domination, when the MAS government took office in 2006 it not only failed to break with extractivist industries, it actually intensified them. A primary objective of the government's economic strategy was to nationalize extractive and refinement industries, in particular those involving hydrocarbon, and to use part of the profits to fight poverty by funding health, education, and other social programs along with subsidies, which has been an extraordinary success. In this respect, however, neither the structure of the national economic formation nor the nature of its integration into the world market were radically transformed. The government was following, in effect, a two-step strategy like the one delineated by early dependency theorists, according to which the export of primary products would allow the importation of "capital goods" needed for development.[1] Although the practices and aspirations of dependency theorists (such as "import substitution") and the corresponding notion of development continue to characterize the MAS economic policy, even in the current government of Luis Arce, the second step of the strategy (instantiated, for instance, by the national industrialization plan) has materialized so far only in fragmentary form. This means, as Franck Poupeau observes, that even the "plurality of economy," which figures prominently in the program of the MAS, is "relegated to the background."[2]

In Bolivia, as in several other Latin American countries, the continued prominence of extractive activities in the economic programs of "progressive" governments has engendered heated opposition regarding "extractivism" or "neo-extractivism."[3] Even the TIPNIS conflict, which we mentioned earlier, has often been framed in such terms since the highway would facilitate extractive activities. Critiques of extractivism and developmentalist discourses raise important questions. Some variants of that critique, sometimes in the name of mitigating climate change or restoring the natural environment, go so far as to oppose extraction itself. It would be more beneficial instead, in our view, first to focus on "purely extractive" economies, to take a phrase from the work of the great pan-African thinker Walter Rodney; that is, destructive, static, oligarchic formations, with corrupting impli-

---

[1] See Raúl Prebisch, *The Economic Development of Latin America and Its Principal Problems* (New York: United Nations, 1950), 2.

[2] Franck Poupeau, *Altiplano. Fragments d'une revolution* (Paris: Raisons d'agir, 2021), 369.

[3] For instance, see Thea Riofrancos. "*Extractivismo* Unearthed: A Genealogy of a Radical Discourse." *Cultural Studies* 31:2–3 (2017), 277–306.

cations for the entire social and political system.[4] Moreover, the point is to ask, on the one hand, *to which aims* extraction is performed, which raises questions regarding the form of economic development, and, on the other, *how* extraction is performed, which raises ecological questions.

Our approach to the discourses critical of modern forms of economic development is similar to our stance regarding those critical of extractivism. We share the primary arguments posed by critiques of development elaborated over the last few decades by scholars such as Arturo Escobar, particularly with respect to Latin American traditions of "developmentalism" (*desarrollismo*) nurtured by dependency theories. And we agree on the need to challenge the projection of a linear path linking modernization, progress, and development. And yet, this does not lead us to argue against development *as such*. A first step is to separate the concept of development from that of growth and the increased consumption of material goods, as it has often traditionally been defined—while keeping in mind, of course, that the fight against poverty inevitably requires, at least in the short term, providing the poor greater access to commodities. Rather than abandoning the concept of development, we are convinced of the need to rethink it and examine the alternative potentials that it contains. In current debates surrounding such notions as "ecomodernism," "ecosocialism," and "degrowth" we should emphasize the political dimension of the struggle around the production, appropriation, and distribution of social wealth. One essential criterion by which to measure alternative development, for example, should be the extent to which it enhances social cooperation under conditions of freedom and equality.

---

[4] Walter Rodney, *How Europe Underdeveloped Africa* (London and Dar-Es-Salaam: Bogle-L'Ouverture Publications, 1973), 106.

This would have to transform existing patterns of consumption, shifting the social divisions that have traditionally defined who has access to commodities. And such cooperation would necessarily change also the dynamics of extractive and industrial processes. In short, economic development must be intrinsically tied to social development.

Lithium production provides an opportunity to work through these questions regarding extraction and development. On one hand, since it requires extractive and refinement processes like other metals, lithium appears to be part of the traditional economic development model. On the other hand, lithium figures prominently among the so-called "transition minerals," that is, raw materials that are key both to the ecological and the digital transition that promise to transform the global economy in the next decades. Lithium batteries are key to powering electric vehicles in particular, but also all sorts of digital devices. To be clear, we do not believe that lithium batteries will fix such a complex problem as climate change, and we are aware that many current forms of ecological and digital transition are themselves ecologically damaging, unsustainable in the long term, and constitute terrains for the extension of the operations of capital. We fully recognize that one should not unquestioningly accept processes that reproduce colonial relations of extraction and that engage in the global capitalist economic framework. Our point is rather that such a double transition must become a field of struggle. Bolivia's vast reserves of lithium (according to some estimates, among the largest in the world), along with a rapidly growing global demand and a consequent high price for lithium, provide an extraordinary opportunity. One must keep in mind, of course, that the demand and price of lithium is likely to be volatile in coming years, depending in part on the possible development of alternative battery technologies. Nonetheless, it is important to ask whether Bolivia can play a prominent role in the global digital and ecological transition, and simultaneously challenge the position assigned to the country by the supposedly rigid international divisions of labor and power. We take lithium both as a concrete opportunity for Bolivia and as an instance of the possibility to imagine development beyond established modern (industrial) models and even beyond the supposed rigidities of the international division of labor, which were not significantly challenged by the MAS in the first years of their government. We are aware that such an ambitious project requires momentous struggles and transformations within the capitalist world system, a long-term process whose conditions are complex and do not depend on the initiative of a single national government. It is from this viewpoint that a deepening of regional integration in Latin America builds a first, necessary step, since it would consolidate a negotiating power and would lay the basis for a more favorable management of relations of exchange and cooperation at the level of the world economy.

The fact that Bolivia's reserves of lithium are vast does not mean they are easily accessible for transport and sale. Moreover, lithium extraction carries significant ecological challenges. In Bolivia, lithium is extracted from high-altitude salt flats, which are fragile ecosystems particularly with respect to the balance between fresh and salt water that allows for the reproduction of a significant biodiversity. Indigenous communities in the Department of Potosí (where most reserves of lithium are located) continuously demand to be fully informed about the potential consequences of extraction and to be involved in governmental decisions.

The process of extraction and refinement is complex. It begins with pumping water into salt flats to obtain a brine that contains a mixture of lithium and other elements. The brine is then held in immense ponds so that, slowly, sunshine will evaporate the liquid. Subsequently, refinement processes separate lithium from the other elements in the composite mixture in order to produce, eventually, lithium carbonate, the marketable commodity. The natural environment poses some obstacles to this process in Bolivia. At the Salar de Uyuni, which is the largest reserve of lithium in the country, rain from December to March interrupts the evaporation process. In addition, the use of large quantities of water to produce the brine poses a serious ecological and social challenge. Technological obstacles also limit production. Using Bolivia's current technology, the process is not only slow, but also fails to achieve the most desirable product. At present, Bolivia exports lithium carbonate that is 98.5 percent pure, the "industrial grade" commodity, but is unable to produce "battery grade" lithium carbonate, which must be 99 percent pure. The issues raised by lithium production clearly pose the two questions we asked earlier: "to which aims" and "how" extraction is performed. New technologies could, on the one hand, make lithium extraction faster and environmentally more sustainable and, on the other, generate lithium carbonate of greater purity, which would make export more profitable and, eventually, could lay the basis for the production of lithium batteries in Bolivia, fulfilling the "industrialization of lithium" that has often been announced by Evo Morales as a goal of the MAS government.

In order to overcome or mitigate the technological obstacles, as well as the social and environmental challenges, however, new technologies, patents, and capital are needed, which Bolivia cannot acquire without involving private and foreign actors. And yet, opening the industry in this way requires coming to grips with capitalist logics, rationalities, and operative models outside national and state control. Such challenges, indeed, confront many states in Latin America and beyond that seek to initiate a process of economic transition today, a leap in development that could contribute to creating greater freedom and equality.

The choices, of course, are not limited to either national autarchic development or ceding control to the world market. Indeed, in 2018 the Morales government attempted another path when it established a public-private "mixed company" with a German consortium of auto manufacturers and other companies. Lithium extraction and refinement to "battery grade" material would take place in Bolivia (in accordance with EU environmental regulations) with the provision that 51 percent of the enterprise would remain under Bolivian state control with a Bolivian manager. The Germans would provide technology that would recycle the water employed in the brine for agricultural use, addressing one important environmental challenge, and significantly speed up the process. Correspondingly, battery production would take place in Germany in cooperation with auto manufacturers with 49 percent Bolivian ownership. The endeavor was a creative effort to overcome the impasse of lithium development in Bolivia, which, of course, carried all the risks of engaging in the kind of public-private partnership typical of neoliberal capitalist arrangements. Unfortunately, however, the project became a casualty of the political tensions surrounding the 2019 coup. Morales abrogated the contract with the German consortium in early November 2019, a few days before the coup, in an (ultimately futile) attempt to placate antagonistic political forces in Potosí that had opposed the project. It may be difficult at this point to resurrect the agreement and give the German corporations necessary assurances. We do not know whether a "mixed company" and a public-private partnership, like the arrangement posed by the accord with the German consortium, would ultimately be a successful endeavor, but we are convinced that breaking from the established development models and experimenting with alternatives are necessary to overcome the technological obstacles that are holding back the potential of Bolivia's lithium production, along with the social, political, and economic transformations it could foster.

One potential alternative, which is more ambitious but certainly would lead, if feasible, to greater rewards, is to reorganize lithium production as a project of regional or continental cooperation in a global conjuncture, in which the geography of lithium extraction and battery supply chain is changing rapidly, with China keeping a dominant position. Bolivia, Chile, and Argentina all have great lithium reserves, and thus one could imagine that the three countries of the "lithium triangle" might benefit by sharing technology, logistical networks, and other infrastructures. Regional cooperation in this regard, however, is particularly challenging due to the fact that, whereas it is publicly owned in Bolivia, in Chile and Argentina private corporations dominate lithium extraction and processing (although the Boric government in Chile has proposed opening some public mines). Bolivia has faced particularly fierce competition from the Chilean Corporation SQM (Sociedad Quimica y Minera), which has used its technical and environmental advantages to sell at a lower price. Despite such obstacles, the Bolivian government could take the initiative and propose forms of cooperation that would benefit all its regional partners. Combining their forces could allow them all not only to produce "battery grade" lithium carbonate, but also to initiate the production of lithium batteries, something that neither Argentina nor Chile has been able to accomplish. Thinking further out and even more ambitiously, such cooperative production of lithium and batteries could be extended along the continental supply chain, converting the established auto production facilities in countries like Mexico, Brazil, and

Argentina to electric vehicles. Such a project of continental cooperation would be, admittedly, a bold endeavor with many obstacles, but it is the kind of vision that can give real content to the potential of alternative development.

Rethinking development and opening alternative paths, however, is not just a matter of technology and capital. Political conditions are essential, starting with the mobilization of sections of the population willing to produce and appropriate new social wealth. There are, of course, numerous conditions for ecological, feminist, and Indigenous struggle that must be addressed. Let us indicate here just one area, which we mentioned earlier, in which these conditions are already being established in Bolivia. One of the great social projects accomplished by the Morales/García Linera government was to make public education, including university, free to all. The free university policy, which led to vast increases in enrollments and graduates, especially among the poor and Indigenous, has resulted in the creation of a kind of mass intellectuality, that is, a large stratum of highly educated youth. Thus far the social and economic frameworks of the country have not shifted enough to accommodate and take advantage the talents of these new university graduates, who experience difficulty finding jobs adequate to their abilities. It is not difficult to recognize in them a great untapped potential. Various forms of alternative development could certainly open new employment possibilities, but it should above all be driven by the movements and behaviors of this mass intellectuality itself. Using state funds derived from lithium production, for example, not only for subsidies, which continue to be urgently needed, but also for promoting a digital and ecological transition would be an important step in the direction of producing a leap in development beyond the current impasse in Bolivia and elsewhere in Latin America.

PART II
INDIGENOUS POLITICS, DECOLONIZING SOCIETY, AND THE STATE

DECOLONIZING THE STATE and society has been a central priority and a signature project of the MAS governments over the past fifteen years—a project conducted at both symbolic and material levels, which, of course, are often inextricably mixed. These efforts have resulted in great achievements, and, in some cases precisely because they have been so successful, have also engendered new challenges for moving forward. It is worth reflecting at this point on what notion of decoloniality was contained in the various governmental projects over these years and whether a somewhat different conception of decoloniality might be mobilized today to relaunch these efforts in a conjuncture that appears to many observers also in this respect, characterized by an impasse.

The drafting and approval of the 2009 Constitution was a crucial step in this process. We already stressed that the simple shift from the designation of Bolivia as a "republic," which is understood as perpetuating the legacy of colonial structures and the racial hierarchies of white rule, to a "plurinational state," which affirms Indigenous identities and connotes majority rule, carries not only great symbolic weight but also significant material consequences. The simple affirmation that all are equal before the law, although it may sound, a bland liberal dictum, is a common, widely visible slogan that seems to be imbued with great political significance as a counter to the long traditions of structural racial hierarchies. The Constitution also provides for limited autonomy for some Indigenous nations, although thus far it has been applied to fewer nations than originally expected. The Constitution is widely recognized as providing a structure within, which the decolonization project can take place.

One great sea change, which dovetails with the constitutional process, has been the radically transformed racial composition of those in power, a point that we mentioned in the first section of this essay, but that needs to be stressed again. This is clearly visible, for example, in the membership of the legislative assembly, both the lower chamber and the senate, which have gone from majority white to majority Indigenous (along with a dramatic gender shift due to the guarantee of parity between male and female representatives). In addition to the legislative assembly, Indigenous populations have entered into all the administrative positions of national, regional, and municipal government, as well as nongovernmental, activist groups that regularly collaborate with government decision-making. One might say that, accompanying and reinforcing the fact that the plurinational state recognizes the rights of Indigenous populations, the state, under the MAS government, is also increasingly managed by Indigenous actors.

It is difficult to measure shifts in racial consciousness, but it is clear that in the last fifteen years there has been a rapid transformation of cultural images, with the affirmation of Indigenous identities and the decline of previously prevalent racist stereotypes. Far from remaining frozen in ancestral times, Indigenous cultural identities have proven flexible and mobile over the last fifteen years. Once the colonial and postcolonial mechanisms of subjugation were challenged and at least partially broken, a new field of subjectivation emerged. Already a few years after the "gas war," researchers described the "multiple identities" of Aymara youth in El Alto, combining "elements of Indigenous, miners, peasants, *gremial* tradition in a modernized urban context, where modern practices (e.g., the use of Internet) intermingle with ancestral values."[5] This process has continued to unfold in the following years, while it has taken different forms in different sites and Indigenous nations. To a certain extent, one can say that undermining denigrating racial stereotypes and affirming Indigenous culture and values have destroyed the homogenous conception of the Indian and made more visible a proliferation of Indigenous identities, among ethnic communities and within each one.

The economic empowerment of different Indigenous populations has been equally significant. Various union structures, such as peasant unions, as we said earlier, have a much greater voice in government decision-making and have in many cases been incorporated into government structures with an institutional role. Indigenous groups have also taken a greater entrepreneurial role, and this is one terrain on which new and unexpected tensions among Indigenous populations have arisen. In part, this is due to the simple fact that increasing economic power can lead to greater conflicts among economic interests. Two different Indigenous groups of coca growers in the Chapare region, near Cochabamba, for example, compete over market access, and if

---

[5] Florencia Puente and Francisco Longa, "El Alto: Los dilemas del indigenismo urbano. Entre la insurrección y el clientelismo*" in Bolivia: Memoria, insurgencia y movimientos sociales*, eds. Maristella *Svampa and Pablo Stefanoni* (Buenos Aires: El colectivo, 2007), 115.

the government supports the claims of one group over the other, the tensions are further inflamed. Another, more complex example involves the commercial ambitions and successes of a portion of the Aymara population. Although the Aymara have a long tradition of commercial activity, the economic power of some Aymara merchants has expanded manyfold, in part through the general processes of political and economic empowerment, resulting in an emerging Indigenous capitalist class. The ostentatious new mansions in El Alto of the *Q'amiri* (the wealthy merchants we will mention again in the next section) serve as a symbol for some of how Indigenous entrepreneurs are wielding economic power as new capitalists. The expression of anticapitalist antagonism within Indigenous communities against such newly emergent capitalist strata is an inevitable result of this process.

One global axis of tension among Indigenous populations, which has its own history but has gained visibility and importance with the increased focus on ethnic identity and Indigenous empowerment, is expressed as resentment to Andino-centrism, that is, the predominance of the two largest ethnic groups, Aymara and Quechua, located primarily in the highlands, over the numerous smaller groups largely in the lowlands (while the position of the Guaraní in the south east is in many respects a different matter). The TIPNIS conflict that we mentioned earlier, in which highland Indigenous populations either sided with the government or simply refrained from supporting the small Indigenous groups directly affected, was one instance in which this axis of inter-Indigenous tension came to the fore.

One could say that these various forms of conflict among Indigenous groups is itself a sign of success of efforts for Indigenous empowerment, although the results have been unequal and often not accompanied by anticapitalist efforts.

Even to the extent that this is the fruit of empowerment, there is obviously need to confront and address the remaining and new challenges.

The most dangerous and volatile result of successful Indigenous empowerment has been the increasing resentment of white populations who have suffered a loss of privilege and thus believe they are aggrieved. The scenario is familiar in situations where progress has been accomplished toward undoing structures of racial subordination—anti-Black violence in the US, at least since Emancipation perpetuated by whites who have lost privilege, is a paradigmatic example. In Bolivia the resentment of white populations in response to the empowerment and progress toward equality of Indigenous populations, has been simmering at least since the election of Evo Morales. The proceedings of the Constituent Assembly in Sucre in 2006–2007, when the structures of a plurinational state were being worked out, generated particularly intense racist expressions of resentment. Members of the constituent assembly and right-wing politicians felt licensed to proclaim out loud, in opposition to the constitution, all kinds of racist tropes that usually remain simmering under the surface of political discourse.

During the coup d'état in 2019 and throughout the period of de facto government, however, white resentment and violence reached a boiling point. Populist crowds and right-wing politicians, while insisting that the election had been stolen through fraud, demanded explicitly that Bolivia be taken back by the real Bolivians, that is, the white population. Their direct objective was to dismantle the plurinational state and return to the republic, which served as thinly veiled code for white rule. The burning of the Wiphala flag in front of the Government Palace, which we mentioned earlier, along with videos of police officers taking the Wiphala flag off of their uniforms, were particularly potent symbols of this explicit racist counter-offensive. We said earlier that the various right-wing forces were never able to come together either in elections or in the period of de facto government. The one thing that still today most unites them, however, which runs throughout their populist rhetoric and inspires the violence of right-wing gangs and paramilitary groups, is white resentment at the loss of privilege.

In such a violent context, in which the substantial gains toward racial equality and democracy are threatened, it may be difficult to focus on what seems to us the crucial questions that Bolivia faces at this point. Some activists believe that the return of the right-wing's explicitly racist rhetoric and action during the coup and de facto government, destructive and violent as it has been, also has had a positive effect: to remind the Bolivian people who is the primary enemy and that the major line of conflict is between the forces of white supremacy and the Indian. The hope, in this regard, is that such a reminder will re-set the political landscape and re-energize a united Indigenous political program, pushing to the background the relatively minor conflicts among different Indigenous groups.

We agree that clarifying battle lines in this way has a positive effect, but it also seems important to us that there be a reckoning regarding the differences between the current conjuncture and when Morales took office—differences due, as we said, in large part to the progress made during these years. One should first ask, what was meant by decolonization in 2006 and to what extent has that project been accomplished? Although asking that question could lead toward a project of completing the process, it may be more useful to question further and ask, what does decolonization mean now? The accomplishments of the past fifteen years have brought Bolivia to a new point, from which a greater vision may be possible. A point of departure today, for example, which seems central to the agenda of many activists, may be to link together *lo popular* and indigeneity, and thus to challenge together class and racial/ethnic hierarchies, that is, to link more strongly Indigenous empowerment and collective anticapitalist struggle. A more challenging task, but no less urgent and already active in incipient forms, would be to make feminist objectives more central to Indigenous struggles—feminist objectives, of course, not dictated by foreign NGOs, but that emerge directly within the movements. Finally, it may also be essential now to frame decoloniality beyond national borders and the struggle for Indigenous liberation at a regional or even continental level. Today's task, in other words, might be one aimed at not completing the project launched earlier, but enacting a rupture and setting off on a somewhat new course.

PART III
STATE, PARTY, AND
SOCIAL MOVEMENTS

As a whirlwind of insurgency swept Latin America beginning in the 1990s, powerful social movements, with different modes of contesting the "Washington consensus" and neoliberalism in each country, played a key role in preparing the ground for the first wave of progressive governments. Venezuela's *Caracazo*, the great revolt of the poor in Caracas in 1989, the Indigenous uprisings in Ecuador starting in 1990, and the Argentinean insurrection in December 2001, are just three of a wide array of social movements that helped topple reactionary, neoliberal regimes and prepare the ground for change. (The Zapatista rebellion in Mexico beginning in 1994 played a unique role at the regional and global level, providing new political languages and imaginaries.) Although the relationship between them was not direct, linear, or unproblematic, the progressive governments in the region were inextricably tied to the movements and struggles that established their conditions of possibility.

The insurgent social movements in Bolivia during those years were in many respects consistent with those elsewhere in Latin America, but also, in some regards, exceptional. Bolivia's long history of rebellion, which had been centered on Indigenous struggles and workers' struggles, underwent a significant shift in the 1990s, with the emergence of new organizational forms and discourses of Indigenous politics, as well as new modes of dialogue between Indianism and Marxism. The MAS, which was refounded in 1997 with Evo Morales' leadership, emerged from this process and gave expression to the range of anti-neoliberal movements, including the coca-leaf growers, *cocaleros*, who had become an important component of the tumultuous rebellion. Two massive struggles against the privatization of social resources were turning points in the insurgency: the so-called "water war" in Cochabamba in 2000, followed by the "gas war" in El Alto three years later, which, after days of open confrontation and over eighty dead, led to the resignation of President Gonzalo Sánchez de Losada. Although one should by no means credit the MAS with the success of those uprisings, the party certainly played a role. Furthermore, one can recognize a direct line between the uprisings and the MAS's electoral victory in December 2005.

When the MAS was refounded in 1997, a suffix was added to the name, MAS-ISP, to indicate that the party is now an "instrument for popular sovereignty." This self-definition configures the party not (or not only) as representative of the people in struggle but as a tool that the struggles themselves can wield. This is the sense in which the MAS government presents itself as a government of social movements. Indeed, daily consultations and negotiations with the major social movements supporting the MAS, in particular those participating in the National Coordination for Change (CONALCAM), established in 2007, significantly shaped Bolivian governmental politics in subsequent years. Such close collaboration and incorporation of movements within governmental structures, with varying degrees of autonomy, has profoundly altered the political and social landscape of the country.

The incorporation of key social movements into state structures, however, has been double-edged. Some lament that the movements have been coopted by the state, which is true to an extent; but in other respects, the state has equally been coopted by the movements. Greater access to and coordination with governmental organizations have increased the power and resources of many social movements and even given them limited influence over the state. This has been notable, as we mentioned earlier, in various processes of Indigenous empowerment and the "Indianization" of the state. However, it has also resulted in a process of not only the institutionalization and bureaucratization of the movements, but also their depoliticization, reducing their capacity to innovate and conduct actions antagonistic to the party and the state. This is one manifestation, as Raquel Gutiérrez Aguilar argues, of "the tensions between what was partly a successful advance into electoral territory by the social struggle and the state political dynamics" in the realm of the liberal electoral system.[6] Throughout the years of the MAS government, this has been an important terrain of struggle.

In order to better understand this process, we should begin with the fact that a high degree of institutionalization is not completely new to these movements. And this fact is even more pronounced because in Bolivia the guild (*gremial*) model has predominated within social movements, tending toward forms of negotiation that reproduce the corporative structure. Rural peasant unions, for instance, which play an important role in

---

[6] Raquel Gutiérrez Aguilar, *Rhythms of the Pachakuti: Indigenous Uprising and State Power in Bolivia*, trans. Stacey Alba D. Skar, (Durham: Duke University Press, 2014) 94.

Bolivia, have long been highly organized and institutionalized in this way. This is equally true of urban Indigenous movements, in which the Inca community form of the *ayllu*, although radically transformed and updated in many respects, continues to shape important organizations, such as the Federation of neighborhood committees (FEJUVE) of El Alto. That said, however, the forms of institutionalization have changed significantly. Whereas neighborhood committees (*juntas vecinales*) in El Alto in the 1950s, for instance, served to compensate for the absence of state structures in the provision of basic social services; today, even though they still conceive of themselves as social movements, these committees form an integral part of governmental structures, both increasing their power, as we said, and multiplying the conditions for bureaucratization. (Perhaps the traditional notion of "social movement" itself fits uneasily with the basic characteristics—the social composition, the capacity to mobilize and forward demands, and the power to innovate politically—of these forms of social organization and action.)

It is important, when interpreting the landscape of today's social movements, that we do not use maps from the past. Our maps need to be updated due, in large part, to the successful projects the government has conducted. Over the last fifteen years, new patterns of consumption, new identities, new social needs, and new subjectivities have emerged in both rural and urban contexts. We mentioned earlier one important example of these transformations: free access to higher education has greatly increased the number of college graduates and dramatically changed the composition of the student body in public universities, increasing the number of Indigenous and poor students, and thus undermining in part the historically rooted privileges of the wealthy white minority. As has happened in many other countries, this massification and democratization of higher education has led, in the absence of wider transformations of the economic and social systems, to a large pool of university graduates who cannot find, in the narrow labor market, employment adequate to their skills. Another facet of this new landscape, which we mentioned in the last section, results from policies that have empowered Indigenous populations in economic and political life, which has led to forms of diversification and even fragmentation of cultural identities, resulting at times in increased conflicts within and among Indigenous communities. We view as symptomatic of the wider changes the formation of a stratum of Aymara capitalists (*Q'amiri*) with newfound commercial power.

Many tend, when trying to grasp the contours of the new map of the social landscape, to invoke the notion of a (new) middle class, but, in the current situation, reference to the middle class obscures more than it illuminates. It does helpfully indicate, no doubt, the increased purchasing power and political role of the poor, along with the increased complexity of social stratification after fifteen years of MAS government policies. Middle class in this sense implies a relative distance or estrangement from popular politics and needs—from the "national popular," to use the Gramscian concept that René Zavaleta Mercado creatively reinvented and adapted to Bolivian history and conditions. It is important to keep in mind, however, that the notion of the middle class has long been used, particularly in the US, to theorize (and contribute to) a process of the normalization of social behaviors. Indeed, one effect of speaking of a new middle class can be to obscure the high degree of heterogeneity among the emerging social subjectivities in terms of not only "objective" position within economic structures, but also "subjective" needs, behaviors, and imaginaries. Rather than the homogenizing effect of the concept of middle classes, what is needed is the means to differentiate and, thus, to discover potentialities for a new politics of socialist transformation in the present conjuncture.

Recognizing and valorizing the new social composition that has emerged from fifteen years of MAS government could, in fact, be key to renewing the political dynamic of social movements with respect to the state, creating new spaces for contestation and a greater degree of autonomy. This new social composition has the capacity both to transform "historical," established movements already structurally embedded within state institutions, and to foster new movements that engage the current relations of force. The point is not to extricate the movements from governmental relations—because, indeed, as we said, the dynamic between the state and social movements has in many respects been very productive—but rather to reset the relationship in different terms, creating the conditions for a new cycle of popular mobilization and governmental invention. In particular, such a change could break the vicious cycle of bureaucratization and depoliticization of both social movements and the state, which, has been a strong contributing factor to the current impasse. The example we cited earlier of a new collective intelligence fostered by free access to higher education is, admittedly, just one instance but, nonetheless, a potent one that indicates the potential for new struggles to further deepen socialist politics in Bolivia.

Hand in hand with what we have called bureaucratization is the increasingly corporativist orientation of many social movements, limited to the interests of their own social sector. One negative effect of this process, in addition to reducing the potential for cooperation among movements, is that these movements increasingly rely on the state and the party to provide the general, strategic perspective—another face of the depoliticization we mentioned earlier. This arrangement runs counter to some of the most original aspects of both the insurgent movements in the early 2000s, when the movements were deeply engaged in developing the overall strategic project, the MAS sharing with them that responsibility. Today's guild-like segmentation of the movements and their reliance on the strategic capacities of the state is another face of the current political impasse. A breakthrough, a new phase of political innovation is needed to open a further stage of the socialist project.

Feminist movements can and should play a central role in this process. Gone are the days when feminism could be dismissed merely as an issue for NGOs and the urban "middle classes." Indeed, the emergence of "popular feminism" in Bolivia, as in other Latin American countries, has dramatically changed the picture. Bolivian feminist movements are not as massive or developed as in some neighboring countries, such as Argentina, but their role and power is increasing, especially that of Indigenous feminisms. Keep in mind that one of the first mass protests against the "de facto" government in 2020 was the feminist demonstration on March 8th from El Alto to La Paz, and that the 2022 March 8th demonstrations were multitudinous all over the country, mixing joyous rebellion with indignation against feminicide and gender violence. The continuity of feminist mobilization, which can never be appropriated or fully represented by a government or a party, can help to weave together different movements and struggles, multiplying their power, and contributing in an original way to the reinvention of the politics of intersectionality that has characterized several Latin American countries in recent years.

The political innovation and the breakthrough, however, must not only arise from the movements but also come from above. Of course, the protagonism of the poor and the Indigenous must be central, as in the earlier phase, along with feminist and other insurgent subjects that have emerged in recent years. But one cannot simply wait for a new wave of insurrectionary uprisings, like those of the early 2000s, as if it were a bolt of lightning, an event from the outside. The MAS may be an instrument of popular sovereignty as its name says, but it is not a passive tool. It has the capacity to initiate and launch a new political project. This is a wealth that was not present in the early 2000s. We are not saying that the movements should bow to the authority of the party and simply follow its lead (further deepening the current state of depoliticization). A repoliticization of the movements, as we said, requires regaining autonomous initiative, working simultaneously with and against the party and the state. To break through the impasse, in other words, and this is the great possibility we see emerging on the horizon, political innovation is required from above and from below, working in *antagonistic cooperation*. This is how we understand the politics of autonomy today: neither a static principle that can engender a sort of identity politics within movements nor something definable exclusively in social terms (usually characterized by hostility toward any engagement with institutions). We see autonomy rather as a flexible criterion of political action and organization that emphasizes the power of movements and struggles to drive processes of social transformation, establishing a wide range of relations with existing institutions, with different measures of antagonism and cooperation. What matters most is that movements and struggles retain their capacity for independent decision-making and action, which builds the very condition for political creativity and innovation. It is not clear that the MAS in its current configuration is up to the task of taking the initiative to enable such antagonistic cooperation, inventing a new project, while engaging productively with newly politicized movements. That is one of the key challenges ahead.

CONCLUSIONS: IMPASSE AND RUPTURE

THINKING THE WORLD from Bolivia was the title of a series of seminars in La Paz organized by the vice presidency that began in 2007 and, with invited foreign speakers, aimed to highlight the role of Bolivia and the MAS government in progressive political processes in a larger frame. Bolivia provides a privileged standpoint, the project proposed, for understanding the present conjuncture at a global scale. Fifteen years later, in a very different conjuncture, both for Bolivia and the wider continental and global scene, we find it useful to return to that proposition. In this essay we have primarily focused on Bolivia and its social, economic, and political developments, the significant successes accomplished along with the weaknesses and new challenges that have been revealed. At the same time, as we learn from Bolivia we have the world in mind, the tumultuous and conflictual world we inhabit, torn by wars, threatened by reactionary political forces, poisoned by patriarchal and racist social structures, imperiled by climate disaster, and more. We take seriously, in other words, even if it remains in the background, the challenge to think the world from Bolivia. Although we have remained close to the Bolivian situation in this text, our aim when analyzing the impasse in that country has also been to contribute to understanding and overcoming a more general impasse of the political imagination of the left.

More directly, and this can be a step toward the larger context, our aim is to grasp the current Bolivian situation in a continental frame. Many have remarked, as we said at the outset, that, given the electoral victories of the left in Chile in 2021, together with Colombia and Brazil in 2022, along with the return to power of the MAS government in Bolivia, we may be in the midst of a second wave of progressive governments in Latin America. There are, no doubt, strong countervailing forces in play—the defeat of the proposed Constitution in Chile was a strong setback and the election of Lula in Brazil was closer than expected—but it would be a mistake to discount the potential of the current progressive forces, in each country and at a regional level.

We are not academic specialists of Latin America, but over the last twenty years we have learned from activists and scholars in the region and we have assiduously followed the vicissitudes of the progressive governments. Our writings have been deeply influenced by such conversations and study, and we have often used fragments (and sometimes more than fragments) of Latin American theories or experiences to make sense of global processes and political challenges. This approach continues to shape our work, as should be clear also from this text. First of all, we attempt to learn from such complex and articulated political experiences as the Bolivian ones, and we try to produce resonances with other experiences that in the best case can illuminate both. Our own positions and modest proposals emerge from such an interplay as well as a constant dialogue with a wide array of interlocutors. Latin America today seems to be in a state of uncertain and turbulent transition, haunted by forces of the right and open to the potentiality of a new wave of socialist political innovation. Bolivia provides an effective angle on such a predicament, first of all because the left has remained in power for more than fifteen years, with the relatively brief break of the coup and the "de facto" government.

Nevertheless, we have the impression that the impasse of the government of Morales and García Linera in its final years, which we elaborated on earlier, has not been overcome by the new administration led by President Luis Arce. It seems to us that the MAS continues to read Bolivian reality without sufficiently taking into account the mutations of the "political anatomy" of society and economy that have been largely engendered by its governmental action. In this context, the question of development becomes a central political issue. Although we fully oppose the forms of development past and present that have wrought so much ecological and social damage, particularly those engaged in extractivist practices, we are not in favor of abandoning the concept of development as such. Instead, we maintain that development, even development that incorporates some extractivist practices, should be an object of debate and struggle again. The case of lithium in Bolivia, although there remain numerous political and technological obstacles to overcome, has the potential to break the rigidities of the world market and the international division of labor while valorizing some of the social forces that have emerged over the last fifteen years and opening a path toward renewed projects of socialist politics.

One political condition for such a project would be creating a new assemblage of the relations between state and social movements. For this it may be necessary to rethink the very notion of social movements, and this is again a wider concern that takes peculiar forms in the Bolivian situation. What matters for us most is an understanding of movements and struggles that keeps the space open for the emergence of processes of politicization involving the new subjectivities that shape the Bolivian social landscape today. The point is not to somehow "substitute" old, established subjects with new, presumably "more advanced" ones, but rather to forge new coalitions capable of combining the claims of heterogeneous subjects, pushing the action of the government in ways that are not necessarily free of friction, antagonism, and even direct conflict. The history of Bolivia since the late 1990s demonstrates that moments of insurgent politics are key to opening new political horizons and laying the groundwork for innovative governmental policies. This dynamism between insurgency and governance has been lost in recent years, and that is at least one of the factors that in our view constitutes the impasse of the MAS. Breaking the double process of bureaucratization and depoliticization that has enveloped both the state and social movements is clearly a crucial condition for moving forward. And this also regards the field of Indigenous politics insofar as the decolonization processes that are in many ways the hallmark of the MAS that need to be reframed and deepened.

The state has a crucial role to play in the process of transition, but it is equally important to establish and valorize the conditions for autonomous and antagonistic mobilizations and struggles. Far from weakening or destabilizing the government's position, such autonomy would make the government stronger and, in particular, more effective at confronting the threats coming from the right. Needless to say, we do not pretend to have recipes to offer. We are focused rather on the ongoing debate within the government, the party, and some of the major movements to find a way to break what is widely perceived as an impasse and to create the conditions for moving forward toward a new phase of socialist politics.

Inventing such a new phase and creating the conditions needed to realize it are necessary at the regional level, and they constitute prerequisites for truly launching a second wave of progressive governments in Latin America. Such a second wave could, perhaps, hold the potential to launch new processes of cooperation and integration and presage the emergence of a progressive bloc in a world that is more and more characterized by what Adam Tooze calls "centrifugal multipolarity."[7] But regional cooperation is also essential for the further development within each national context. Thinking of the regional frame as a constitutive component of a new political project, not just an additional level to be addressed after national political issues are resolved, can lay the foundations for the success of the political experiments that are needed to advance toward a new socialist politics. We know that this project faces strong headwinds and that there are uncertainties and pitfalls ahead. But betting on such a prospect, and acting to make it real, is crucial in the current conjuncture of global politics.

---

[7] Adam Tooze, *Shutdown: How Covid Shook the World's Economy* (London: Allen Lane, 2021), 294.

BIBLIOGRAPHICAL NOTE

For readers who would like to explore these themes further, the following texts have proven especially useful for us.

A good starting point is The Bolivia Reader. History, Culture, Politics, *ed. by S. Thomson, R. Barragán, S. Qayum, and M. Goodale, Durham, NC: Duke University Press, 2018. René Zavaleta Mercado's writings on Bolivian history, society, and politics provide an essential guide: see for instance the collection of his essays,* Horizontes de visibilidad. Aportes latinoamericanos marxistas, *Madrid: Traficantes de sueños, 2021 and, in English,* Towards a History of the National Popular in Bolivia, *London and Calcutta, Seagull Books, 2018. Álvaro García Linera is also an important reference to understand the politics of the MAS and the process of transformation of the last fifteen years: see for instance his* Plebeian Power: Collective Action and Indigenous, Working-Class and Popular Identities in Bolivia, *London, Brill, 2014* [originally La potencia plebeya. Acción colectiva e identidades indígenas, obreras y populares en Bolivia, *Buenos Aires, Prometeo, 2010.*] *For a snapshot of the revolutionary conjuncture of the 2000s see Forrest Hylton,* Revolutionary Horizons: Past and Present in Bolivian Politics, *London – New York: Verso, 2007. An excellent account and an in-depth discussion of the questions raised by the Bolivian revolution is provided by the book by Franck Poupeau,* Altiplano. Fragments d'une revolution, *Paris, Raisons d'agir, 2021.*

On the so-called "Pink tide," the progressive governments in Latin America in the first long decade of the 21st century, see for instance Franck Gaudichaud, Massimo Modonesi, and Jeffery R. Webber, The Impasse of the Latin American Left. *Duke University Press (Radical Américas), 2022* [*originally* Los gobiernos progresistas latinoamericanos del siglo XXI. Ensayos de interpretación histórica, *México, UNAM Ediciones, 2019*] *and Steve Ellner,* Latin America's Pink Tide: Breakthroughs and Shortcomings, *New York: Rowman & Littlefield, 2019. On the relations between social movements and progressive governments, as well as on the politics of autonomy, see Verónica Gago and Sandro Mezzadra,* "In the Wake of the Plebeian Revolt. Social Movements, 'Progressive' Governments, and the Politics of Autonomy in Latin America." Anthropological Theory, *17 (2017), 4: 474–496.*

On the 2019 coup an excellent analysis is provided by the 12 chapters of the audiovisual essay by Verónica Córdova, Noviembre rojo, *available on YouTube. See also Jorge Viana,* "Bolivia: la contrarrevolución de noviembre y la ineficacia de la revolución," *in* Estados alterados, *ed. by C. Bautista, A. Durand, and H. Ouviña, Buenos Aires: Clacso, 2020; and Bruno Bosteels, "A Militarized Stalement in Bolivia," Commune, 22 November 2019, https://communemag. com/a-militarized-stalemate-in-bolivia.*

For the critical discussion of development in Latin America the work of Arturo Escobar is an essential reference: see his Encountering Development. The Making and Unmaking of the Third World, *Princeton, NJ: Princeton University Press, 2012. A book we mention in the section on development, which does not directly discuss Bolivia but remains methodologically important is the classical work by Walter Rodney*, How Europe Underdeveloped Africa, London and Dar-Es-Salaam: Bogle-L'Ouverture Publications, 1973. *For the reference to "ecomodernism," "ecosocialism," and "degrowth," an article by Kai Heron is a good starting point: see "The Great Unfettering,"* Sidecar, *7 September 2022, https://newleftreview.org/sidecar/posts/the-great-unfettering.*

The critical literature on extractivism in Latin America is very wide, including works by well-known scholars like Maristella Svampa and Eduardo Gudynas. A good starting point is the double issue of the journal Cultural Studies *on extractivism (31, 2017, 2–3), and in particular the essay by Thea Riofrancos, "Extractivismo unearthed: a genealogy of a radical discourse," 1–30.*

On Indigenous politics, again, debates and texts abound (not to mention the historical and anthropological background of the issue). An important figure in the recent history of Indianismo *is Felipe Quispe Huanca: see for instance his* Mi militancia. MITKA, Movimiento Indio Tupaj Katari, *La Paz: Ediciones Pachakuti, 2018. For a critical analysis of* Indianismo, *see the book by Pedro Portugal Mollinedo and Carlos Macusaya Cruz,* El indianismo katarista. Una mirada crítica, *La Paz: Fundación Friedrich Ebert, 2016. An interesting angle on decolonization and education is provided by Jiovanny Samanamud Ávila, "Interculturalidad, educación y descolonización,"* Integra educativa, 3 (2010), 1: 67–80. *Among the several books on decolonization in Bolivia, see Rafael Bautista S.,* La descolonización de la política. Introducción a una política comunitaria, *Cochabamba: AGRUCO, 2014.*

On social movements in Bolivia the existing literature is again very wide. The best resource in English regarding the social movements between 2000 and 2005 is Raquel Gutiérrez Aguilar, Rhythms of the Pachakuti: Indigenous Uprising and State Power in Bolivia, *trans. Stacey Alba D. Skar, Durham: Duke University Press, 2014. A good starting point in Spanish is the book edited by Pablo Stefanoni and Maristella Svampa,* Bolivia: Memoria, Insurgencia y Movimientos sociales, *Buenos Aires: El Colectivo – Clacso, 2007 (we quote in the article a chapter of this book, written by Florencia Puente and Francisco Longa, "El Alto: los dilemmas del indigenismo urbano. Entre la insurreción y el clientelismo," 97–123). The work of the* Colectivo comuna *(1999–2010) is particularly important in this respect: see for instance R. Gutiérrez, Á. García Linera, R. Prada, and L. Tapia,* Democratizaciones plebeyas, *La Paz: Muela del Diablo Editores 2002. See also the latest book of the collective, on the state and its relation with social movements: Á. García Linera, R. Prada, L. Tapia, and O. Vega Camacho,* El estado. Campo de lucha, La Paz: Muela del Diablo, 2010.

On Bolivian feminism, see for instance the work of Adriana Guzmán Arroyo within the network "Feminismo comunitario antipatriarcal": Descolonizar la memoria, descolonizar los feminismos, *https://www.biodiversidadla.org/Documentos/Descolonizar-la-memoria-descolonizar-los-feminismos. A relevant book is the one recently published by María Galindo from the collective "Mujeres creando,"* Feminismo bastardo, *Madrid: Traficantes de sueños, 2021.*

ABOUT THE AUTHORS

Michael Hardt teaches political theory in the Literature Program at Duke University. He is co-author of several books with Antonio Negri, including *Empire*. His most recent book is *The Subversive Seventies*. Together with Sandro Mezzadra, he hosts The Social Movements Lab.

Sandro Mezzadra teaches political theory at the University of Bologna, Department of Arts. His most recent book in English is *In the Marxian Workshops: Producing Subjects* (2018). With Brett Neilson, he is the author of *Border as Method, or, the Multiplication of Labor* (2013) and *The Politics of Operations: Excavating Contemporary Capitalism* (2019).

ABOUT COMMON NOTIONS

COMMON NOTIONS IS a publishing house and programming platform that fosters new formulations of living autonomy. We aim to circulate timely reflections, clear critiques, and inspiring strategies that amplify movements for social justice.

OUR PUBLICATIONS TRACE a constellation of critical and visionary meditations on the organization of freedom. By any media necessary, we seek to nourish the imagination and generalize common notions about the creation of other worlds beyond state and capital. Inspired by various traditions of autonomism and liberation—in the US and internationally, historical and emerging from contemporary movements—our publications provide resources for a collective reading of struggles past, present, and to come.

COMMON NOTIONS REGULARLY collaborates with political collectives, militant authors, radical presses, and maverick designers around the world. Our political and aesthetic pursuits are dreamed and realized with Antumbra Designs.

WWW.COMMONNOTIONS.ORG
INFO@COMMONNOTIONS.ORG

MORE FROM
COMMON NOTIONS

19 and 20: Notes for a New Insurrection
Colectivo Situaciones

With Contributions by Marcello Tarì, Liz Mason-
Deese, Antonio Negri, and Michael Hardt
Translated by Nate Holdren and Sebastian Touza

ISBN: 978-1-942173-48-9 (print)
ISBN: 978-1-942173-62-5 (eBook)
$20.00 | 6 x 9 | 288 pages
Subjects: Latin America/Insurrections/Resistance

**From a rebellion against neoliberalism's miser-
able failures, notes for a new insurrection and a
new society.**

19 and 20 tells the story of one of the most popular uprisings against neoliberalism: on
December 19th and 20th, 2001, amidst a financial crisis that tanked the economy, ordinary people in Argentina took to the streets shouting "¡Qué se vayan todos!" (They all
must go!) Thousands of people went to their windows banging pots and pans, neighbors
organized themselves into hundreds of popular assemblies, workers took over streets and
factories. In those exhilarating days, government after government fell as people invented
a new economy and a new way of governing themselves.

It was a defining moment of the antiglobalization movement and Colectivo Situaciones
was there, thinking and engaging in the struggle. Their writings during the insurrection
have since been passed hand to hand and their practice of militant research modelled
widely as a way of thinking together in a time of rebellion. Today, as a staggering debt
crisis deepens, we see the embers from that time twenty years ago in the mutual aid initiatives and new forms of solidarity amidst widespread vulnerability.

Revisiting the forms of counterpower that emerged from the shadow of neoliberal rule,
Colectivo Situaciones reminds us that our potential is collective and ungovernable.

MORE FROM
COMMON NOTIONS

Grupo de Arte Callejero: Thought, Practices, and Actions
Grupo de Arte Callejero

Translated by the Mareada Rosa Translation Collective

ISBN: 978-1-942173-10-6 (print)
ISBN: 978-1-942173-34-2 (eBook)
$22.00 | 6 x 9 | 352 pages
Subjects: Art/Latin America/Social Theory

An indispensable reflection on what was done and what remains to be done in the social fields of art and revolution.

Grupo de Arte Callejero: Thought, Practices, and Actions tells the profound story of social militancy and art in Argentina over the last two decades and propels it forward. For Grupo de Arte Callejero [Group of Street Artists], militancy and art blur together in the anonymous, collective, everyday spaces and rhythms of life. Thought, Practices, and Actions offers an indispensable reflection on what was done and what remains to be done in the social fields of art and revolution.

Every new utopian struggle that emerges must to some extent be organized on the knowledge of its precedents. From this perspective, Grupo de Arte Callejero situates their experience in a network of previous and subsequent practices that based more on popular knowledge than on great theories. Their work does not elaborate a dogma or a model to follow, but humbly expresses their interventions within Latin American autonomous politics as a form of concrete, tangible support so that knowledge can be generalized and politicized by a society in movement.

Without a doubt this will not be the most exhaustive book that can be written on the GAC, nor the most complete, nor the most acute and critical, but it is the one GAC wanted to write for themselves.

MORE FROM
COMMON NOTIONS

Genocide in the Neighborhood: State Violence, Popular
Justice, and the 'Escrache'
Colectivo Situaciones
Translated by Brian Whitener

ISBN: 978-1-942173-86-1 (print)
ISBN: 978-1-945335-02-0 (eBook)
$20.00 | 6 x 9 | 128 pages
Subjects: Latin America/Insurrections/Resistance

Documents the theories, debates, successes, and failures of a rebellious tactic to build popular power.

Genocide in the Neighborhood documents the autonomist practice of the "escrache," a system of public shaming that emerged in the late 1990s to vindicate the lives of those disappeared under the Argentinean dictatorship and to protest the amnesty granted to perpetrators of the killing.

Through a series of hypotheses and two sets of interviews, *Genocide in the Neighborhood* documents the theories, debates, successes, and failures of the escraches—what Whitener defines as "something between a march, an action or happening, and a public shaming—investigates the nature of rebellion, discusses the value of historical and cultural memory to resistance, and suggests decentralized ways to agitate for justice.

The book follows the popular Argentine uprising in 2001, a period of intense social unrest and political creativity that led to the collapse of government after government. The power that ordinary people developed for themselves in public space soon gave birth to a movement of neighborhoods organizing themselves into hundreds of popular assemblies across the country, the unemployed workers struggle mobilizing, and workers taking over factories and businesses. These events marked a sea change, a before and an after for Argentina that has since resonated around the world. In its wake *Genocide in the Neighborhood* tactfully deploys a much needed model of political resistance.

BECOME A COMMON NOTIONS MONTHLY SUSTAINER

These are decisive times ripe with challenges and possibility, heartache, and beautiful inspiration. More than ever, we need timely reflections, clear critiques, and inspiring strategies that can help movements for social justice grow and transform society.

Help us amplify those words, deeds, and dreams that our liberation movements, and our worlds, so urgently need.

Movements are sustained by people like you, whose fugitive words, deeds, and dreams bend against the world of domination and exploitation.

For collective imagination, dedicated practices of love and study, and organized acts of freedom.
By any media necessary.
With your love and support.

Monthly sustainers start at $12 and $25.

commonnotions.org/sustain

Printed in the USA
CPSIA information can be obtained
at www.ICGtesting.com
JSHW080006150824
68134JS00021B/2313

9 781942 173977